simple pasta

simple pasta

This edition first published in the U.K. in 1999 by Hamlyn for WHSmith, Greenbridge Road, Swindon SN3 3LD

Printed in China

ISBN 0 600 598918

Notes

1 Standard level spoon measurements are used in all recipes.

1 tablespoon = one 15 ml spoon
1 teaspoon = one 5 ml spoon

2 Both imperial and metric measurements have been given in all recipes. Use one set of measurements only and not a mixture of both.

3 Eggs should be medium unless otherwise stated. The Department of Health advises that eggs should not be consumed raw. This book may contain dishes made with lightly cooked eggs. It is prudent for more vulnerable people, such as pregnant and nursing mothers, invalids, the elderly, babies and young children, to avoid uncooked or lightly cooked dishes made with eggs. Once prepared, these dishes should be used immediately.

4 Milk should be full fat unless otherwise stated.

5 Fresh herbs should be used unless otherwise stated. If unavailable, use dried herbs as an alternative but halve the quantities stated.

6 Ovens should be preheated to the specified temperature – if using a fan-assisted oven, follow the manufacturer's instructions for adjusting the time and the temperature.

7 Pepper should be freshly ground black pepper unless otherwise stated; season according to taste.

8 This book includes dishes made with nuts and nut derivatives. It is advisable for customers with known allergic reactions to nuts and nut derivatives and those who may be potentially vulnerable to these allergies, such as pregnant and nursing mothers, invalids, the elderly, babies and children, to avoid dishes made with nuts and nut oils. It is also prudent to check the labels of pre-prepared ingredients for the possible inclusion of nut derivatives.

9 Vegetarians should look for the 'V' symbol on a cheese to ensure it is made with vegetarian rennet. There are vegetarian forms of Parmesan, feta, Cheddar, Cheshire, red Leicester, dolcelatte and many goats' cheeses, among others.

contents

introduction

Pasta has been a staple food for thousands of years. Records show that the Chinese were eating pasta as far back as the Shang dynasty some 3,500 years ago. However, it is the Italians who are the most serious pasta eaters. It is not hard to see why pasta is so popular as it's the most versatile convenience food ever. Cheap, quick and easy to cook – and perfectly designed to mix with anything from a drizzle of olive oil and a sprinkling of herbs, to colourful ingredients like olives and tomatoes, or thick sauces made with sausage or smoked fish – pasta can be served as a starter or main course, and used in many different types of dishes, from soups to salads.

Pasta is made from wheat flour and water. The best Italian varieties use durum wheat, a hard wheat which makes a good firm pasta dough. Some doughs are made with eggs and these pastas are called *pasta all'uovo*. When spinach is added to the dough, it is called *pasta verde*, and when tomato is included the pasta is called *pasta rossa*. Wholewheat pasta and buckwheat pasta are also available; both these pastas have a brown colour and a more chewy texture and are richer in vitamins, minerals and fibre.

Types of pasta

Pasta is readily available fresh or dried, in an enormous variety of shapes and sizes. Dried pasta, called *pasta secca* in Italian, is particularly useful as it can be stored for months in the kitchen cupboard. It ranges in size from tiny shapes, called pastini, to the large cannelloni tubes, which are ideal for stuffing. The recipes in this book use dried pasta unless fresh is specified. Fresh pastas include ribbon pastas such as tagliatelle, linguine and spaghetti, and sheets of pasta for lasagne and cannelloni. Fresh stuffed pastas such as ravioli and tortellini are also now sold in most supermarkets.

The following are just some of the many varieties of pasta available.

Bucatini: thick, tubular spaghetti. Good with thick and smooth sauces.

Cannelloni: large, hollow tubes for stuffing with meat, fish or vegetables. Can be baked in a sauce.

Capelli d'angelo: also called angel hair; long, very thin vermicelli. Good with smooth sauces and in soups.

Conchiglie: shells in many different sizes. Use with chunky and creamy sauces, and in soups and salads.

Farfalle: also called bows; available fresh or dried. May be flavoured with spinach or tomato. Use with sauces and in salads.

Fedelini: also called spaghettini; long, thin spaghetti. Use with smooth and creamy sauces.

'No man is lonely while eating spaghetti;
it requires so much attention.'

Christopher Morley

Fettucine: long, flat ribbon noodles, sometimes coiled into nests. Use with smooth and creamy sauces.

Fiorelli: short tubes, one end having a lacy edge. Good with chunky sauces.

Fusilli: spirals, coils or springs, long or short; available fresh or dried; may be flavoured with spinach. Use with sauces and in salads.

Gnocchi: small potato dumplings eaten in the same way as pasta.

Lasagne: flat rectangular or square sheets; sometimes ridged or with crinkled edges. Available fresh or dried; may be flavoured with spinach. 'No pre-cook' lasagne is also available. Use in layers with meat, fish or vegetables and cheese sauce in baked dishes, or rolled around filling to make cannelloni.

Linguine: thin, flat ribbon noodles. Use like spaghetti.

Lumache: snails. Use like conchiglie.

Macaroni: thick, slightly curved, hollow pasta of varying lengths, such as short-cut and elbow macaroni. Quick cook macaroni is also available. Use with thick and creamy sauces; good in baked dishes.

Noodles: there are numerous types of oriental noodles made from wheat flour but they tend to be paler in colour than Italian varieties. Thin white noodles are made from rice flour or mung bean flour. Can be used in soups and sauces, or stir-fried.

Pappardelle: broad egg noodles made in a similar way to tagliatelle, but cut into wider strips. Use like tagliatelle.

Pastini: tiny shapes (for example, anelini, conchigliette, farfallette, orecchiette, and roteline). Use in soups, casseroles and children's dishes.

Penne: short, tubular quills with angled ends. Penne rigate are ridged. Use like short-cut macaroni.

Ravioli: fresh pasta filled with spinach and ricotta cheese. Serve with melted butter or a sauce.

Rigatoni: short-cut, ridged tubes. Use like short-cut macaroni.

Rotelle: also called ruote; shaped like cartwheels or wagon wheels. Good for children's dishes, and in soups, stews and salads.

Spaghetti: long, thin strings, available fresh or dried. Spaghettini is thinner. Use with any kind of sauce.

Tagliarini: flat ribbon noodles, thinner than tagliatelle, available fresh or dried. May be flavoured with tomato, spinach and egg.

Tagliatelle: flat ribbon noodles, sometimes coiled into nests, available fresh or dried. May be flavoured with herbs, spinach or egg. Good with smooth sauces.

Tortellini: Small, stuffed shapes of fresh pasta with fillings such as tomato and basil. Tortelloni are the same shape only larger. Serve with melted butter or sauce.

Tripolini: small, rounded bows. Good in soups.

Vermicelli: thin pasta strands. Use like spaghetti.

Servings
As a rough guide, allow 75–125 g (3–4 oz) fresh or dried pasta per person for a main course; 50 g (2 oz) for a starter. The amount depends on whether the pasta is to be served simply or with a substantial sauce.

Cooking pasta
Pasta is very easy to cook as long as you follow a few simple rules. The most important one is that pasta must be cooked in a large saucepan in plenty of boiling, salted water, so that it has room to cook without sticking together. Try to use a saucepan which will hold at least 4 litres (7 pints) of water. You can add a little olive oil to the water, if you like – opinions differ as to whether this helps to prevent the pasta strands or shapes from sticking together. When cooking spaghetti, add it all to the pan at the same time, gently pushing the pasta into the boiling water as it softens.

Give the pasta a good stir and maintain it at a steady boil while it is cooking. Fresh pasta will take 2–3 minutes (5–10 minutes for filled types); dried pasta takes 8–12 minutes though you should always check the packet instructions and test the pasta for readiness a little before the suggested time. Pasta is ready when it is al dente, an Italian term meaning tender but still firm when bitten. Test by biting a piece or squeeze a piece of it between your fingers; if it breaks cleanly, it is cooked. Do not cook pasta until very soft or it will be mushy by the time you serve it.

Dry pasta swells to almost double its original bulk during cooking so drain it in a colander. Serve cooked pasta at once.

quick & easy

mushroom & boursin tagliatelle

1 Bring a large saucepan of salted water to the boil. Add the pasta and cook for 8–12 minutes or according to the packet instructions, until just tender.

2 Meanwhile, make the sauce. Heat the oil in a pan and fry the onion and garlic until softened. Add half the chives with the mushrooms and wine. Bring to the boil and cook for 2 minutes, then remove from the heat, stir in the boursin and cream and season to taste. Stir until heated through.

3 Drain the pasta, add it to the sauce and toss gently to combine everything. Serve garnished with the remaining chives.

375 g (12 oz) spinach tagliatelle

1 tablespoon olive oil

1 onion, chopped

2 garlic cloves, crushed

2 tablespoons snipped chives

250 g (8 oz) button mushrooms, sliced

125 ml (4 fl oz) dry white wine

50 g (2 oz) boursin cheese with pepper

125 ml (4 fl oz) double cream

salt and pepper

Serves 4

Preparation time: 10 minutes

Cooking time: 8–12 minutes

1 Bring a large saucepan of salted water to the boil. Add the pasta and cook for 8–12 minutes or according to the packet instructions, until just tender. Drain and run under cold water until the pasta is cold.

2 Blanch the mangetout and asparagus in a saucepan of boiling water for 2 minutes, then drain in a colander. Refresh under cold water, then add to the bowl of pasta with the carrot, spring onions and the red pepper.

3 In a small, heavy-based saucepan, heat the sesame and sunflower oils. Add the ginger and sesame seeds and cook for 30–60 seconds until they start to pop. Remove the pan from the heat, stir in the soy sauce and season to taste with salt and pepper. Pour the dressing over the pasta and toss thoroughly. Serve immediately.

300 g (10 oz) caserecce

150 g (5 oz) mangetout, trimmed

100 g (4 oz) asparagus tips, halved widthways

1 large carrot, cut into matchsticks

4 spring onions, cut into matchsticks

2 red peppers, cored, deseeded and cut into strips

2 tablespoons sesame oil

2 tablespoons sunflower oil

2.5 cm (1 inch) piece of fresh root ginger, peeled and finely shredded

2 teaspoons sesame seeds

50 ml (2 fl oz) soy sauce

salt and pepper

Serves 4
Preparation time: 10 minutes
Cooking time: 8–12 minutes

oriental caserecce

macaroni with sausage & tomato

1 Break each sausage into 4 or 5 pieces. Heat the oil in a large saucepan, add the garlic and onions and cook them until softened and lightly coloured.

2 Add the sausages and fry until evenly browned. Add the red peppers, tomatoes, oregano, tomato purée, Marsala or sherry and salt and pepper to taste. Cook gently, uncovered, for 12–15 minutes.

3 Meanwhile, bring a large saucepan of salted water to the boil. Add the pasta and cook for 8–12 minutes or according to the packet instructions, until just tender. Drain well and stir in the butter.

4 Mix the pasta and sauce together and transfer to a warmed serving dish or individual dishes. Serve at once.

250 g (8 oz) Italian sausages, skinned

2 tablespoons olive oil

2 garlic cloves, peeled and crushed

2 small onions, peeled and roughly chopped

2 small red peppers, cored, deseeded and cubed

750 g (1½ lb) tomatoes, skinned and chopped

2 teaspoons dried oregano

2 tablespoons tomato purée

6 tablespoons Marsala or sherry

250 g (8 oz) macaroni

25 g (1 oz) butter

salt and pepper

Serves 4
Preparation time: 20 minutes
Cooking time: 20 minutes

■ Italian pork sausages, called *salamelle*, have a coarser texture and stronger flavour than British sausages. They can be fried or boiled.

penne with spicy olive sauce

1 Bring a large saucepan of salted water to the boil. Add the pasta and cook for 8–12 minutes or according to the packet instructions, until just tender.

2 Drain the pasta and return it to the pan. Add the oil, the ginger, nutmeg, garlic, capers, olives and chopped parsley.

3 Season with salt and pepper and stir over a low heat for 1–2 minutes. Serve at once, garnished with basil sprigs.

500 g (1 lb) penne

125 ml (4 fl oz) olive oil

½ teaspoon ground ginger

pinch of freshly grated nutmeg

1 garlic clove, crushed

3 tablespoons capers

75 g (3 oz) pitted black olives, sliced

2 tablespoons chopped parsley

salt and pepper

basil sprigs, to garnish

Serves 4

Preparation time: 10 minutes

Cooking time: 10–15 minutes

16

1 Soak the anchovy fillets in a little milk for a few minutes to remove the excess salt. Heat the oil in a small pan. Add the whole garlic clove and the drained anchovies. Cook over a medium heat for a few minutes, then remove the garlic and add the bacon.

2 Meanwhile, drain the tomatoes and cut into strips. When the bacon is crisp, add the tomatoes to the pan. Season with salt and pepper and leave to cook over a low heat for about 10 minutes. Add the olives and oregano and continue cooking until a thick sauce has formed.

3 Bring a large saucepan of salted water to the boil. Add the pasta and cook for 8–12 minutes or according to the packet instructions, until just tender. Drain the pasta and transfer to a warmed serving dish, then pour on the sauce and sprinkle with the grated pecorino cheese. Mix well before serving.

2 anchovy fillets

a little milk

4 tablespoons oil

1 garlic clove

50 g (2 oz) smoked bacon, derinded and diced

425 g (14 oz) can plum tomatoes

50 g (2 oz) pitted black olives, chopped

¼ teaspoon chopped oregano

375 g (12 oz) macaroni

25 g (1 oz) pecorino cheese, grated

salt and pepper

Serves 4

Preparation time: 10–15 minutes

Cooking time: 25–30 minutes

country-style macaroni

quick pasta soup

1 Heat the oil in a large saucepan, add the onion, parsley, vegetables and tomato purée and cook for 2 minutes, stirring.

2 Add the hot vegetable stock and bring to the boil. Add the pasta, lower the heat and simmer, covered, for about 8–12 minutes or until the pasta is cooked.

3 Add plenty of salt and pepper to taste. Serve at once with some crusty bread.

1 tablespoon olive oil

1 onion, chopped

2 tablespoons chopped parsley

250 g (8 oz) diced mixed vegetables

2 tablespoons tomato purée

1.2 litres (2 pints) hot vegetable stock

50 g (2 oz) conchiglie

salt and pepper

crusty bread, to serve

Serves 4
Preparation time: 2–3 minutes
Cooking time: 10–14 minutes

smoked chicken & penne rigate

1 Bring a large saucepan of salted water to the boil. Add the pasta and cook for 8–12 minutes or according to the packet instructions, until just tender.

2 Meanwhile, heat the tablespoon of oil in a frying pan and add the shallots. Fry for 1 minute, stirring constantly, until softened. Add the mushrooms and fry for 2 minutes more. Reduce the heat and add the cheese, breaking it up with the back of a wooden spoon. Stir in the double cream, chicken and parsley. Stir over a low heat for 5 minutes until thoroughly heated through. Add plenty of salt and pepper to taste.

3 Drain the pasta and drizzle with a little oil. Season with pepper and add to the sauce. Stir well and then serve at once.

■ The chestnut mushroom is a variety of the common cultivated mushroom, with a strong flavour. If unavailable, use ordinary button mushrooms.

375 g (12 oz) penne rigate

1 tablespoon olive oil, plus extra for drizzling

2 shallots, finely chopped

125 g (4 oz) chestnut mushrooms, sliced

150 g (5 oz) soft cheese with herbs

150 ml (¼ pint) double cream

250 g (8 oz) smoked chicken breast, skinned and sliced

2 tablespoons chopped parsley

salt and pepper

Serves 4	
Preparation time:	10 minutes
Cooking time:	8–12 minutes

penne with turkey & pesto

1 Bring a large saucepan of salted water to the boil. Add the pasta and cook for 8–12 minutes or according to the packet instructions, until just tender.

2 Heat a wok or large, deep frying pan and add the oil. Heat until it is hot, but not smoking. Add the turkey and stir-fry for 1–2 minutes. Add the pesto and stir-fry for a further 1–2 minutes until the turkey is thoroughly heated through.

3 Drain the pasta, add it to the turkey mixture and toss over a high heat until well mixed. Add the cream or crème fraîche and season to taste with salt and pepper. Toss well to mix, then divide between 4 warmed serving plates. Garnish with Parmesan shavings and basil and serve at once.

300 g (10 oz) penne

1 tablespoon olive oil

375 g (12 oz) cooked turkey, cut into thin strips

3 tablespoons ready-made pesto

4–6 tablespoons double cream or crème fraîche

salt and pepper

To Garnish:

Parmesan cheese shavings

basil leaves

Serves 4
Preparation time: 5 minutes
Cooking time: 10–14 minutes

spaghetti with genovese sauce

1 Put the garlic cloves, walnuts, basil leaves, Parmesan and oil into a blender or food processor and blend until smooth. Season to taste with salt. Alternatively, use a pestle and mortar to pound the garlic with a little salt, then add the walnuts and then the basil, pounding between each addition to form a smooth purée. Add the cheese and oil and stir well.

2 Bring a large saucepan of salted water to the boil. Add the pasta and cook for 8–12 minutes or according to the packet instructions, until just tender.

3 Drain the pasta, return it to the rinsed-out pan and stir in half the sauce. Pile the pasta onto a warmed serving dish and serve garnished with basil leaves. Hand the rest of the sauce separately.

3 garlic cloves

40 g (1½ oz) walnuts

25 g (1 oz) basil leaves, finely chopped, plus extra to garnish

50 g (2 oz) Parmesan cheese, grated

150 ml (¼ pint) olive oil

375 g (12 oz) spaghetti

salt

Serves 4

Preparation time: 15 minutes

Cooking time: 8–12 minutes

■ This delicious sauce will keep for up to 2 weeks in a screw-top jar in the refrigerator.

fresh pasta with crab & courgettes

1 Cut the courgettes into thin strips. Melt the butter in a pan, add the garlic and courgettes and cook for 3 minutes.

2 Meanwhile, bring a large saucepan of salted water to the boil. Add the pasta and cook for 2–3 minutes or according to the packet instructions, until just tender. Drain the pasta and add it to the pan with the courgettes.

3 Add the crab to the pan with the lemon juice and season generously with salt and pepper. Stir the ingredients gently to combine them, then cook over a moderate heat for 1–2 minutes to heat the crab meat. Serve at once, garnished with lemon wedges and parsley sprigs.

250 g (8 oz) courgettes, trimmed

50 g (2 oz) butter

1 garlic clove, crushed

375 g (12 oz) fresh pasta, such as linguine

175 g (6 oz) white crab meat

2 teaspoons lemon juice

salt and pepper

To Garnish:

lemon wedges

parsley sprigs

Serves 4
Preparation time: 10 minutes
Cooking time: 5 minutes

asparagus & mushroom tagliatelle

1 Melt the butter in a large frying pan and add the asparagus, mushrooms and ginger. Mix gently and allow the vegetables to cook slowly, without browning, for 5–8 minutes.

2 Add the tarragon and cream or crème fraîche to the pan. Season to taste with salt and pepper. Stir gently, then simmer for 5 minutes.

3 Meanwhile, bring a large saucepan of salted water to the boil. Add the pasta and cook for 8–12 minutes or according to the packet instructions, until just tender.

4 Drain the pasta and return it to the rinsed-out saucepan. Pour the asparagus and mushroom sauce over the tagliatelle and stir carefully. Transfer to a warmed serving dish and garnish with a few strips of lemon rind and parsley sprigs, if liked. Serve straight away.

25 g (1 oz) butter

250 g (8 oz) fresh asparagus spears, cut into 2.5 cm (1 inch) lengths, blanched

125 g (4 oz) chestnut mushrooms, sliced

2.5 cm (1 inch) piece of fresh root ginger, peeled and grated

1 tablespoon chopped tarragon

250 ml (8 fl oz) double cream or crème fraîche

375 g (12 oz) fresh tagliatelle

salt and pepper

To Garnish:

strips of lemon rind

parsley sprigs (optional)

Serves 4
Preparation time: 10 minutes
Cooking time: 15–20 minutes

1 Bring a large saucepan of salted water to the boil. Add the pasta and cook for 8–12 minutes or according to the packet instructions, until just tender.

2 Meanwhile, heat the oil and the butter in a pan, add the garlic and cook over a moderate heat for 2 minutes. Pour in the stock and sherry and boil rapidly for 5 minutes to reduce the liquid. Stir in the tuna, cream and two-thirds of the parsley. Season with salt and pepper and stir well to mix.

3 Drain the spaghetti and toss with the sauce. Serve garnished with the remaining parsley.

375 g (12 oz) spaghetti

2 tablespoons olive oil

25 g (1 oz) butter

1 garlic clove, finely chopped

200 ml (7 fl oz) fish or chicken stock

3 tablespoons dry sherry

200 g (7 oz) can tuna, drained and flaked

2 tablespoons single cream

3 tablespoons chopped parsley

salt and pepper

Serves 4
Preparation time: 5 minutes
Cooking time: 15 minutes

spaghetti with tuna sauce

500 g (1 lb) tagliatelle verde

1 broccoli head

2 tablespoons olive oil

1 tablespoon chopped fresh root ginger

2 garlic cloves, thinly sliced

125 g (4 oz) button mushrooms, sliced

250 g (8 oz) scallops

175 g (6 oz) cooked peeled prawns

75 ml (3 fl oz) dry sherry

150 ml (¼ pint) single cream

1 teaspoon chopped marjoram

1 teaspoon chopped thyme

salt and pepper

Serves 4–6

Preparation time: 5–10 minutes

Cooking time: 8–12 minutes

1 Bring a large saucepan of salted water to the boil. Add the pasta and cook for 8–12 minutes or according to the packet instructions, until just tender.

2 Meanwhile, break the broccoli into small florets and boil in salted water for 1 minute, then drain and reserve.

3 Heat the oil in a large frying pan, add the ginger and garlic and brown lightly. Stir in the mushrooms, scallops and prawns. Pour over the sherry and boil rapidly until it is reduced to about 2 tablespoons. Add the cream, herbs and salt and pepper to taste. Add the broccoli to the sauce and heat through. Transfer the drained pasta to warmed serving plates, pour over the sauce and serve immediately.

tagliatelle with broccoli, prawns & scallops

pasta classics

baked lasagne

1 To make the white sauce, melt the butter in small saucepan and stir in the flour. Cook over a gentle heat for 1–2 minutes, then remove from the heat. Gradually beat in the milk, then return to a low heat. Cook, stirring all the time, until you have a thickened, smooth sauce. Season with salt, pepper and nutmeg.

2 Butter an ovenproof dish and pour in a little meat sauce. Add a layer of lasagne sheets, then a layer of white sauce and Bel Paese or fontina. Continue to layer the ingredients to fill the dish, finishing with a layer of white sauce.

3 Sprinkle the Parmesan over the top and bake in a preheated oven at 180°C (350°F), Gas Mark 4 for 40–45 minutes. Serve hot, garnished with sprigs of oregano.

1 quantity Meat Sauce (see opposite), cooked for 20 minutes only

250 g (8 oz) 'no pre-cook' or fresh lasagne sheets

375 g (12 oz) Bel Paese or fontina cheese, thinly sliced or grated

2–3 tablespoons grated Parmesan cheese

oregano sprigs, to garnish

White Sauce:

40 g (1½ oz) butter

40 g (1½ oz) flour

600 ml (1 pint) milk

grated nutmeg

salt and pepper

Serves 4
Preparation time: 20 minutes
Cooking time: 1 hour 20 minutes

1 Heat the oil in a saucepan or deep frying pan, add the onion, garlic, bacon, carrot and celery and cook until soft and golden. Add the beef and cook, stirring occasionally, until browned.

2 Add the red wine and bring to the boil. Reduce the heat slightly and cook over a moderate heat until most of the wine has evaporated. Season with salt and pepper.

3 Add the milk and a little grated nutmeg, and stir well. Continue cooking until the milk has been absorbed by the meat mixture. Add the tomatoes, sugar and oregano. Reduce the heat to a bare simmer and cook, uncovered, for about 2–2½ hours until the sauce is well reduced and richly coloured.

4 Bring a large saucepan of salted water to the boil. Add the pasta and cook for 8–12 minutes or according to the packet instructions, until just tender. Drain well and season with pepper. Pour over the meat sauce and serve at once, with the Parmesan handed separately, if using.

4 tablespoons olive oil

1 onion, finely chopped

1 garlic clove, crushed

4 streaky bacon rashers, derinded and chopped

1 carrot, diced

1 celery stick, diced

500 g (1 lb) lean minced beef

150 ml (¼ pint) red wine

125 ml (4 fl oz) milk

freshly grated nutmeg

425 g (14 oz) can chopped tomatoes

1 tablespoon sugar

1 teaspoon chopped oregano

500 g (1 lb) spaghetti

salt and pepper

50 g (2 oz) Parmesan cheese, grated, to garnish (optional)

Serves 4

Preparation time: 15 minutes

Cooking time: 2½–3 hours

spaghetti alla bolognese

1   Put the clams in a large pan with the water. Cook until the shells open, then remove the clams from the shells. Strain the cooking liquid and reserve for later.

2   Heat the oil in a heavy pan, add the garlic and cook gently for 5 minutes. Remove the garlic, then add the tomatoes and the reserved cooking liquid to the pan. Stir and simmer for 20 minutes.

3   Meanwhile, bring a large saucepan of salted water to the boil. Add the pasta and cook for 8–12 minutes or according to the packet instructions, until just tender. Drain thoroughly.

4   Add the clams and parsley to the tomato sauce and heat thoroughly for 1 minute. Pile the spaghetti in a warmed serving dish, add the sauce and a pinch of pepper, and fork gently to mix. Serve at once.

1 kg (2 lb) fresh clams, scrubbed under cold running water

7 tablespoons water

7 tablespoons olive oil

1 garlic clove, peeled and sliced

425 g (14 oz) tomatoes, skinned and mashed

425 g (14 oz) spaghetti

1 tablespoon chopped parsley

salt and pepper

Serves 4

Preparation time: 20 minutes

Cooking time: 40 minutes

spaghetti alla vongole

■ To peel tomatoes, put them in a bowl and cover with boiling water for 15 seconds, then lift out with a slotted spoon and plunge into cold water. Drain them and peel off the skin.

spaghetti alla carbonara

1 Bring a large saucepan of salted water to the boil. Add the pasta and cook for 8–12 minutes or according to the packet instructions, until just tender.

2 Meanwhile, heat the oil in a large heavy-based saucepan. Add the bacon and cook over a moderate heat until cooked and golden brown.

3 Drain the pasta and add it to the bacon. Gently stir in the beaten eggs and cream. Season to taste with salt and pepper. Stir over a very low heat until the egg starts to set.

4 Toss the spaghetti mixture lightly with most of the Parmesan and serve at once while still very hot, sprinkled with the remaining Parmesan and the chopped parsley.

500 g (1 lb) spaghetti

2 tablespoons olive oil

8 streaky bacon rashers, derinded and chopped

3 eggs, beaten

3 tablespoons single cream

50 g (2 oz) Parmesan cheese, grated

salt and pepper

2 tablespoons chopped parsley, to garnish

Serves 4
Preparation time: 5 minutes
Cooking time: 15–20 minutes

fettuccine alfredo

1 Bring a large saucepan of salted water to the boil. Add the pasta and cook for 8–12 minutes or according to the packet instructions, until just tender.

2 Meanwhile, melt the butter in a very large frying pan. Add the onion and garlic and fry over a high heat for 1 minute, stirring constantly.

3 Warm the cream in a saucepan. Pour it over the onion mixture and add the nutmeg. Bring the mixture to the boil, add salt and pepper to taste, then remove from the heat.

4 Drain the pasta and add it to the sauce. Push the pasta to one side of the pan, return it to a low heat and beat in the egg. While the mixture is cooking, add the Parmesan. Stir well and as soon as the cheese has melted, tip the fettuccine onto warmed plates. Serve at once, garnished with parsley.

300 g (10 oz) fettuccine

25 g (1 oz) butter

1 onion, finely chopped

3 garlic cloves, finely chopped

450 ml (¾ pint) single cream

½ teaspoon grated nutmeg

1 egg, beaten

50 g (2 oz) Parmesan cheese, grated

salt and pepper

1 tablespoon chopped parsley, to garnish

Serves 4
Preparation time: 10 minutes
Cooking time: 15 minutes

pasta primavera

1 Bring a pan of water to the boil and cook the green vegetables and carrot separately until tender but still crisp. Transfer each one to iced water to stop the cooking. Drain well and pat dry with kitchen paper.

2 Bring a large saucepan of salted water to the boil. Add the pasta and cook for 8–12 minutes or according to the packet instructions, until just tender.

3 Meanwhile, melt the butter with the oil in a large frying pan over a moderate heat. Add the red pepper and fry for 1 minute. Add the pine nuts and fry for a further 1 minute. Add the cooked vegetables and toss until they are well coated with oil and warmed right through.

4 Drain the pasta and transfer it to a warmed serving bowl. Add the hot vegetables with the shredded lettuce and chives and toss well. Add salt to taste and toss again. Garnish with the parsley, sprinkle with the Parmesan and serve at once.

250 g (8 oz) mangetout, trimmed

250 g (8 oz) fresh asparagus (optional)

175 g (6 oz) thin French beans

1 carrot, cut into thin strips

375 g (12 oz) spaghetti

25 g (1 oz) unsalted butter

4 tablespoons olive oil

1 red pepper, cored, deseeded and diced

2 tablespoons pine nuts, toasted

½ small lettuce, shredded

2 tablespoons snipped chives

salt

To Garnish:

4 tablespoons finely chopped parsley

freshly grated Parmesan cheese

Serves 4–6	
Preparation time: 10 minutes	
Cooking time: 30–40 minutes	

■ Other vegetables could be substituted. Try courgettes, spring greens, fresh peas or broccoli instead, if preferred.

wholewheat spaghetti marinara

1 Bring a large saucepan of salted water to the boil. Add the pasta and cook for 8–12 minutes or according to the packet instructions, until just tender.

2 Meanwhile, heat the oil in a large frying pan, add the onion and fry gently for 5 minutes until softened. Add the wine and garlic and simmer until the liquid is reduced by one-third. Add the cream or crème fraîche, chives, prawns and mussels. Heat through gently and season to taste with salt and pepper.

3 Drain the pasta and divide it between 4 warmed serving plates. Spoon the sauce over the top and sprinkle with chives. Serve the pasta at once, with Parmesan handed round separately.

375 g (12 oz) wholewheat spaghetti

2 tablespoons olive oil

1 onion, chopped

300 ml (½ pint) dry white wine

1 garlic clove, crushed

150 ml (¼ pint) double cream or crème fraîche

2 tablespoons snipped chives, plus extra to garnish

175 g (6 oz) cooked peeled prawns

250 g (8 oz) canned or frozen mussels

salt and pepper

Parmesan cheese, to serve

Serves 4

Preparation time: 10 minutes

Cooking time: 15 minutes

■ Fresh mussels could be used instead. Steam in a little wine until they open, then remove from their shells and use as above.

500 g (1 lb) wholewheat tagliatelle

50 g (2 oz) butter

1 onion, chopped

2–3 garlic cloves, crushed

125 g (4 oz) streaky bacon, derinded and diced

75 g (3 oz) Bel Paese cheese, grated

75 g (3 oz) mature Cheddar cheese, grated

75 g (3 oz) Gruyère cheese, grated

50 g (2 oz) Parmesan cheese, grated

300 ml (½ pint) double cream

2 tablespoons chopped parsley

2 tablespoons chopped chives

1 tablespoon chopped basil

salt

Serves 4–6

Preparation time: 5 minutes

Cooking time: 8–12 minutes

1 Bring a large saucepan of salted water to the boil. Add the pasta and cook for 8–12 minutes or according to the packet instructions, until just tender.

2 Meanwhile, melt half the butter in a saucepan, add the onion and garlic and cook, without browning, for 2–3 minutes. Add the bacon and cook for 5 minutes, stirring occasionally. Stir in the cheeses and cream. Remove from the heat.

3 Drain the pasta thoroughly and turn into a warmed serving dish. Add the remaining butter and toss well. Return the sauce to the heat and stir in the herbs. Pour over the pasta and mix well. Serve immediately.

tagliatelle with four cheeses

1 Bring a large saucepan of salted water to the boil. Add the pasta and cook for 8–12 minutes or according to the packet instructions, until just tender.

2 Meanwhile, heat the oil and the butter in a flameproof casserole, add the onion, carrot and celery, and cook over a low heat for 4 minutes.

3 Add the crumbled sausage, diced pepper and torn basil and mix well. Cook over a moderate heat for 3–4 minutes until the sausage has browned. Add the red wine.

4 Drain the pasta and transfer it to a warmed serving dish. Pour on the sausage and vegetable sauce. Sprinkle with the cheeses and mix well before serving, garnished with whole basil leaves.

3 tablespoons oil

25 g (1 oz) butter

½ onion, chopped

1 small carrot, finely sliced

1 celery stick, sliced

125 g (4 oz) Italian sausage, skinned and crumbled

½ small yellow pepper, cored, deseeded and diced

4 basil leaves, torn

50 ml (2 fl oz) dry red wine

425 g (14 oz) penne

2 tablespoons grated pecorino cheese

2 tablespoons grated Parmesan cheese

whole basil leaves, to garnish

Serves 4
Preparation time: 10 minutes
Cooking time: 8–12 minutes

penne with spicy sausage sauce

smoked haddock & pepper pasta

1 Rinse the haddock then pour boiling water over it and leave for 2 minutes. Rinse again, then put into a pan, cover with the milk and bring to the boil. Reduce the heat and simmer for 10–15 minutes. Strain, reserving the milk, and leave to cool.

2 Heat the oil in another pan, add the shallots and garlic and cook gently for 5 minutes until softened. Add the peppers and cook gently for 5–6 minutes, stirring occasionally.

3 Stir 125 ml (4 fl oz) of the strained milk into the cream, then mix in the cheese. Add more milk if it is too thick: it should be the consistency of double cream. Purée the shallots and peppers with the cheese mixture in a blender or food processor or simply stir the cream into the peppers. Return to the pan and add the tarragon and pepper. Taste the sauce and add the sugar if necessary.

4 Bring a large saucepan of salted water to the boil. Add the pasta and cook for 8–12 minutes or according to the packet instructions, until just tender.

5 Skin, bone and flake the fish. Add it to the sauce and stir well. Drain the pasta and return to the pan with half the butter. Whisk the rest of the butter into the simmering sauce. Pile the pasta into a warmed dish, pour the sauce over and serve at once.

500 g (1 lb) smoked haddock fillets

600 ml (1 pint) milk

2 tablespoons olive oil

3 shallots, finely chopped

2–3 garlic cloves, finely chopped

2 large red peppers, cored, deseeded and finely sliced

4 tablespoons soured cream

125 g (4 oz) low-fat soft cheese

1 tablespoon chopped tarragon

¼–½ teaspoon caster sugar (optional)

250 g (8 oz) farfalle or conchiglie

25 g (1 oz) butter

salt and pepper

Serves 4–6	
Preparation time: 15 minutes	
Cooking time: 40 minutes	

macaroni cheese

1 Bring a large saucepan of salted water to the boil. Add the pasta and cook for 8–12 minutes or according to the packet instructions, until just tender. Drain thoroughly. Return the pasta to the pan, add half the butter and toss to mix.

2 Melt the remaining butter in a pan, add the flour and stir over a low heat for 2 minutes. Gradually stir in the milk and bring to the boil, stirring or whisking constantly. Cook for 2 minutes, then stir in the mustard and Tabasco and Worcestershire sauces. Add the Cheddar and stir until it has melted.

3 Fold in the macaroni. Spoon into a buttered ovenproof dish and sprinkle with the breadcrumbs and Parmesan. Arrange the sliced tomato over the top, if using. Bake in a preheated oven at 200°C (400°F), Gas Mark 6 for 25–30 minutes until hot and golden brown. Serve at once.

250 g (8 oz) short-cut macaroni

50 g (2 oz) butter

25 g (1 oz) plain flour

450 ml (¾ pint) milk

1 heaped teaspoon English mustard

dash of Tabasco sauce

dash of Worcestershire sauce

175 g (6 oz) mature Cheddar cheese, grated

25 g (1 oz) dried breadcrumbs

25 g (1 oz) Parmesan cheese, grated

1 tomato, sliced (optional)

Serves 4

Preparation time: 10 minutes

Cooking time: 40–50 minutes

spinach cannelloni •

spaghetti with olive oil & garlic •

tortellini with ricotta & spinach •

tagliatelle with radicchio & cream •

spinach gnocchi gratin •

wholewheat pasta with broccoli & blue cheese •

aubergine layer bake •

fettuccine with chanterelles •

courgette & red pesto pasta •

no-meat meals

spinach cannelloni

1 Bring a large saucepan of salted water to the boil. Add half the lasagne sheets and cook for 8–12 minutes or according to the packet instructions, until just tender. Remove with a slotted spoon and drain on kitchen paper. Repeat with the rest of the lasagne sheets.

2 Meanwhile, make the filling. Mix the ricotta, spinach, egg, flour and garlic purée in a bowl. Add salt and pepper to taste. Spoon into a piping bag fitted with a large plain nozzle. Set aside.

3 Make the sauce. Heat the oil in a pan and fry the onion until softened. Stir in the passata and herbs and simmer for 5 minutes.

4 Pipe the filling along the width of each pasta sheet then roll them up to make filled cannelloni tubes. Arrange the tubes on the base of a lightly greased 1.8 litre (3 pint) rectangular ovenproof dish. Pour the sauce over the top and cover with the grated mozzarella. Bake in a preheated oven at 190°C (375°F), Gas Mark 5 for 45 minutes.

12 sheets wide spinach lasagne

Filling:

375 g (12 oz) ricotta cheese

125 g (4 oz) frozen chopped spinach, thawed

1 egg, beaten

25 g (1 oz) plain flour

2 tablespoons garlic purée

salt and pepper

Sauce and Topping:

1 tablespoon olive oil

1 onion, chopped

550 g (18 oz) jar passata (sieved tomatoes)

2 teaspoons mixed dried herbs

250 g (8 oz) mozzarella cheese, grated

Serves 4
Preparation time: 20 minutes
Cooking time: 1¼ hours

1 Bring a large saucepan of salted water to the boil. Add the pasta and cook for 8–12 minutes or according to the packet instructions, until just tender. Drain thoroughly.

2 Heat the oil in the empty pasta pan and add the garlic and chillies, if using. Cook over a moderate heat, stirring constantly, until sizzling. Season the oil generously with salt and pepper.

3 Tip the pasta into the pan and toss to coat each strand in the flavoured oil. Serve at once, sprinkled with more pepper.

375 g (12 oz) spaghetti

5 tablespoons extra virgin olive oil

4 garlic cloves, chopped

1–2 dried red chillies, finely chopped (optional)

salt and pepper

Serves 4
Preparation time: 5 minutes
Cooking time: 8–12 minutes

spaghetti with olive oil & garlic

■ It is worth using extra virgin olive oil for this recipe. This type of olive oil is produced from the first pressing of the olives, so it has a lovely green colour and a full flavour.

tortellini with ricotta & spinach

1 Melt half the butter in a large frying pan, add the spinach and toss thoroughly. Season well with salt and pepper. Sauté the spinach for 2 minutes, stirring constantly.

2 Bring a large saucepan of salted water to the boil. Add the pasta and cook for 5–10 minutes or according to packet instructions, until just tender. Drain thoroughly and toss in the remaining butter.

3 Stir the ricotta and half of the Parmesan into the spinach mixture, then stir in the pasta. Transfer to a warmed serving dish, sprinkle with the remaining Parmesan and serve at once.

125 g (4 oz) butter

250 g (8 oz) frozen chopped spinach, thawed

500 g (1 lb) fresh tortellini

125 g (4 oz) ricotta cheese

50 g (2 oz) Parmesan cheese, grated

salt and pepper

Serves 4
Preparation time: 5 minutes
Cooking time: 10–12 minutes

1 Melt the butter with the oil in a large, heavy-based frying pan, add the onion and cook gently for 10 minutes, stirring occasionally, until it is soft.

2 Add the radicchio and cook, stirring, over a moderate heat until it wilts and starts to brown. Season with salt and pepper to taste. Add the cream and heat through.

3 Bring a large saucepan of salted water to the boil. Add the pasta and cook for 2–3 minutes until just tender. Drain the pasta and place in a warmed serving dish. Pour over the sauce and add the Parmesan. Toss quickly to combine and serve at once.

50 g (2 oz) butter

1 tablespoon olive oil

1 onion, finely chopped

250 g (8 oz) radicchio, finely shredded

150 ml (¼ pint) double cream

375 g (12 oz) fresh tagliatelle

50 g (2 oz) Parmesan cheese, grated

salt and pepper

Serves 4

Preparation time: 10 minutes

Cooking time: 15–17 minutes

tagliatelle with radicchio & cream

1 Wash the spinach and remove the stalks, place it in a large saucepan with just the water that clings to the leaves and cook gently for 3–4 minutes until wilted. Drain in a colander, pressing out all the moisture. Chop the spinach finely then put it in the base of a 1.8 litre (3 pint) ovenproof dish and season with salt and pepper.

2 Bring a large saucepan of salted water to the boil, add the gnocchi in batches and cook for just a few minutes. When they pop up to the surface, lift them out with a slotted spoon and drain on kitchen paper. Arrange the gnocchi over the spinach. Pour the tomato sauce over the gnocchi and set aside while preparing the white sauce.

3 Melt the butter in a small saucepan. Add the flour and stir over a low heat for 2 minutes. Stir in the milk and bring to the boil, stirring or whisking constantly. Cook for 2 minutes, then stir in the cambozola and season with salt and pepper. Pour the sauce over the gnocchi. Sprinkle with nutmeg and cook in a preheated oven at 200°C (400°F), Gas Mark 6 for 15 minutes until golden. Serve garnished with radicchio leaves.

400 g (13 oz) fresh spinach

1 kg (2 lb) fresh spinach gnocchi

400 g (13 oz) jar Sugo al Basilico (tomato sauce with basil)

15 g (½ oz) butter

15 g (½ oz) plain flour

300 ml (½ pint) milk

125 g (4 oz) cambozola cheese, crumbled

freshly grated nutmeg

salt and pepper

radicchio leaves, to garnish

Serves 4–6

Preparation time: 5 minutes

Cooking time: 30 minutes

spinach gnocchi gratin

wholewheat pasta with broccoli & blue cheese

250 g (8 oz) wholewheat conchiglie

250 g (8 oz) broccoli, cut into small florets

125 g (4 oz) blue cheese

50 g (2 oz) butter

125 ml (4 fl oz) double cream or crème fraîche

salt and pepper

Serves 4

Preparation time: 5 minutes

Cooking time: 10–15 minutes

1 Bring a large saucepan of salted water to the boil. Add the pasta and cook for 8–12 minutes or according to the packet instructions, until just tender. About 3 minutes before the end of the cooking time, add the broccoli to the pan and cook until both the pasta and the broccoli are tender. Drain well and keep warm.

2 Put the pan back on the heat and add the blue cheese, butter and cream or crème fraîche. Heat gently, stirring all the time to make a smooth sauce. Taste and adjust the seasoning if necessary.

3 Return the pasta and broccoli to the pan, toss thoroughly to mix with the sauce, then turn the mixture on to a warmed serving dish and serve immediately.

2 aubergines, sliced

2 tablespoons olive oil

1 onion, chopped

1 tablespoon chopped oregano

1 tablespoon chopped basil

125 g (4 oz) button mushrooms, cut into quarters

550 g (18 oz) jar passata (sieved tomatoes)

9 fresh lasagne sheets

375 g (12 oz) mozzarella cheese, sliced

125 g (4 oz) Gruyère cheese, grated

salt and pepper

Serves 4
Preparation time: 30 minutes
Cooking time: 1 hour 10 minutes

1 Spread out the aubergine slices on baking sheets. Sprinkle with 25 g (1 oz) salt and set aside for 15 minutes.

2 Heat 1 tablespoon of the oil in a large frying pan. Add the onion and cook for 3–5 minutes, stirring, until softened. Add the herbs, mushrooms and passata. Simmer for 10 minutes, then add salt and pepper to taste.

3 Rinse the aubergine slices under plenty of cold running water, drain and pat dry with kitchen paper. Spread them on the baking sheets and brush with the remaining oil. Grill under a high heat for 10 minutes, turning once. Remove from the heat.

4 Arrange 3 lasagne sheets on the base of a lightly greased rectangular 1.8 litre (3 pint) ovenproof dish. Spoon over one-third of the tomato sauce. Place a layer of aubergines on top, and add one-third of the mozzarella and Gruyère. Repeat the layers twice more. Cover with foil. Bake in a preheated oven at 190°C (375°F), Gas Mark 5 for 45 minutes, removing the foil after 20 minutes to allow the top to brown and the cheese to melt completely.

aubergine layer bake

fettuccine
with chanterelles

1 Thinly slice the chanterelles, reserving any discarded pieces of stem or peel. Pour the stock into a saucepan and bring to the boil. Add the mushroom peelings and cook over a medium-high heat until reduced to 125 ml (4 fl oz). Strain through a sieve and discard the mushroom peelings.

2 Melt the butter with the oil in a large frying pan. Add the mushrooms and spring onions and cook, stirring, until the mushrooms begin to render liquid. Add the wine and cook over a high heat until the liquid has nearly evaporated.

3 Bring a large saucepan of salted water to the boil. Add the pasta and cook for 2–3 minutes or until just tender. Meanwhile, add the reduced stock and cream to the mushroom mixture. Bring to the boil and reduce the sauce to half its original volume. Season to taste with salt and pepper.

4 Drain the pasta, add to the frying pan with the pine nuts and toss to coat evenly with the sauce. Serve at once.

300 g (10 oz) chanterelles, morels or other wild mushrooms

500 ml (17 fl oz) vegetable stock

15 g (½ oz) butter

1 tablespoon olive oil

1 bunch of spring onions, finely chopped

4 tablespoons dry white wine

300 g (10 oz) fresh spinach fettuccine

350 ml (12 fl oz) whipping cream or crème fraîche

2 tablespoons toasted pine nuts

salt and pepper

Serves 4

Preparation time: 15 minutes

Cooking time: 30 minutes

■ Wild mushrooms, which are now widely available in supermarkets and greengrocers, give this dish a wonderful flavour. However, cultivated mushrooms can be used, if preferred.

1 Bring a large saucepan of salted water to the boil. Add the pasta and cook for 8–12 minutes or according to the packet instructions, until just tender.

2 Meanwhile, heat 2 tablespoons of the oil in a deep frying pan, add the garlic, lemon rind, chilli and courgettes and fry for 2–3 minutes until the courgettes are golden.

3 Drain the cooked pasta thoroughly and add to the courgette pan with the remaining oil, the basil, red pesto and plenty of pepper. Toss well over a low heat to warm through gently for 1 minute and serve at once.

375 g (12 oz) penne or other shapes

6 tablespoons olive oil

2 garlic cloves, sliced

1 teaspoon grated lemon rind

1 dried red chilli, deseeded and crushed

500 g (1 lb) courgettes, thinly sliced

1 tablespoon shredded basil leaves

2–3 tablespoons red pesto

salt and pepper

Serves 4

Preparation time: 10 minutes

Cooking time: 10–14 minutes

courgette & red pesto pasta

hearty
dishes

1 tablespoon olive oil

1 garlic clove, crushed

2 onions, sliced into rings

1 teaspoon ground coriander

2 carrots, cut into thin sticks

125 g (4 oz) cooked chicken breast, shredded

1 tablespoon tomato purée

1.2 litres (2 pints) hot chicken stock

75 g (3 oz) conchiglie

75 g (3 oz) mozzarella cheese, cubed

2 tablespoons chopped parsley

1 teaspoon cayenne pepper

salt

crusty bread, to serve (optional)

1 Heat the oil in a large saucepan, add the garlic and onions and cook for 2 minutes, stirring. Stir in the coriander, then add the carrots and chicken. Fry over a moderate heat for 3 minutes.

2 Stir in the tomato purée, stock and a pinch of salt; bring to the boil. Add the pasta, lower the heat and cook for 8–12 minutes or according to the packet instructions, until just tender.

3 Add the mozzarella and parsley, stir well, then sprinkle with cayenne pepper. Serve in heated bowls, with crusty bread, if liked.

Serves 4
Preparation time: 15 minutes
Cooking time: 13–15 minutes

chicken & pasta shell soup

gnocchi & parma ham bake

1 Heat the oil in a large saucepan, add the onion and garlic and cook for 5 minutes, stirring, until softened. Add a pinch of tarragon.

2 Put the drained tomatoes and mascarpone in a food processor and blend to a smooth sauce. Stir the sauce into the onion mixture, add the sun-dried tomato paste and season well. Simmer gently.

3 Bring a large saucepan of salted water to the boil, add the gnocchi in batches and cook for just a few minutes. When they pop up to the surface, lift them out with a slotted spoon and drain on kitchen paper.

4 Transfer the gnocchi to a large ovenproof dish and pour the tomato sauce over them. Stir the Cheddar and breadcrumbs together and scatter the mixture over the top. Tear the Parma ham into thin lengths and lay it over the topping. Scatter over the olives and season again. Sprinkle a little more tarragon on top. Bake in a preheated oven at 180°C (350°F), Gas Mark 4 for 20–25 minutes or until the top is bubbling and golden.

2 tablespoons olive oil

1 red onion, halved and sliced

2 garlic cloves, crushed

2 pinches of dried tarragon

425 g (14 oz) can tomatoes, drained

250 g (8 oz) mascarpone cheese

2 dessertspoons sun-dried tomato paste

500 g (1 lb) fresh gnocchi

125 g (4 oz) Cheddar cheese, grated

50 g (2 oz) fresh white breadcrumbs

75 g (3 oz) Parma ham

10 pitted green olives

salt and pepper

Serves 4

Preparation time: 5 minutes

Cooking time: 35–40 minutes

cannelloni with peas, mushrooms & ham

1 Bring a large saucepan of salted water to the boil, add the lasagne sheets in batches, cook until just tender and drain well. Meanwhile, cook the frozen peas in a pan of boiling salted water according to packet instructions and drain. Melt the butter for the filling in a frying pan, add the mushrooms and fry gently until tender.

2 To make the white sauce, melt the butter in a small saucepan and stir in the flour. Cook gently, stirring, for 1–2 minutes. Remove from the heat and slowly beat in the milk. Return to the heat and bring slowly to the boil, stirring all the time until thick and smooth. Season to taste with salt and pepper.

3 Place 2 tablespoons of the white sauce in a bowl and beat in the egg and the egg yolk. Add two-thirds of the cheese, the ham, peas and mushrooms. Season with salt, pepper and nutmeg to taste, and mix well.

4 Spoon a little of the filling down one long side of each sheet of lasagne and roll up each one into a cylinder. Arrange the cylinders in a buttered, ovenproof dish, coat with the remaining white sauce and sprinkle with the remaining Parmesan. Bake in a preheated oven, 200°C (400°F), Gas Mark 6, for about 20 minutes until the top is golden. Serve hot, garnished with chopped parsley.

12 sheets wide lasagne

parsley, chopped, to garnish

Filling:

125 g (4 oz) small frozen peas

25 g (1 oz) butter

200 g (7 oz) mushrooms, thinly sliced

1 egg, plus 1 egg yolk

75 g (3 oz) Parmesan cheese, grated

200 g (7 oz) lean cooked ham, finely diced

grated nutmeg

salt and pepper

White Sauce:

25 g (1 oz) butter

25 g (1 oz) plain flour

450 ml (¾ pint) milk

Serves 4

Preparation time: 15 minutes

Cooking time: 30 minutes

lasagne marinara

1 First make the sauce. Melt the butter in a saucepan, add the flour and stir over a low heat for 2 minutes. Gradually stir in the milk and bring to the boil, stirring or whisking constantly. Cook for 2 minutes. Pound the saffron strands to a powder with a pestle and mortar and stir in 2–3 tablespoons boiling water until the saffron has dissolved. Add to the sauce and season to taste with salt and pepper.

2 Remove any bones from the salmon and cod and cut the fish into bite-sized pieces. Fold the fish into the sauce with the squid rings. Remove from the heat.

3 Spoon one-third of the fish mixture over the base of a 1.8 litre (3 pint) ovenproof dish, and then cover with a layer of lasagne sheets. Repeat these layers twice, finishing with a layer of pasta sheets. Beat the eggs and Cheddar together in a bowl. Add salt and pepper to taste and pour the mixture over the top of the lasagne.

4 Bake in a preheated oven at 190°C (375°F), Gas Mark 5 for 45 minutes; cover the dish with foil after 30 minutes if the surface starts to overbrown. Serve garnished with dill sprigs.

9 'no pre-cook' lasagne sheets

2 eggs, beaten

200 g (7 oz) Cheddar cheese, grated

dill sprigs, to garnish

Sauce:

50 g (2 oz) butter

50 g (2 oz) plain flour

600 ml (1 pint) milk

a few saffron strands

250 g (8 oz) fresh salmon tail

125 g (4 oz) cod fillet

125 g (4 oz) fresh squid rings

salt and pepper

Serves 4
Preparation time: 10 minutes
Cooking time: 55 minutes

1 Trim the excess fat from the chops. Fry them with the garlic in a non-stick frying pan over a moderate heat for 3 minutes on each side. Transfer the chops to a casserole. Discard any fat remaining in the pan.

2 Melt the butter in the pan, add the courgettes and mushrooms and cook, stirring them once or twice, for 2 minutes. Add them to the chops. Add the tomatoes, honey, wine, marjoram, and salt and pepper to taste. Cover the casserole and cook in a preheated oven at 190°C (375°F), Gas Mark 5 for 25 minutes.

3 About 15 minutes before the chops are ready, bring a large saucepan of salted water to the boil. Add the pasta and cook for 8–12 minutes or according to the packet instructions, until just tender. Drain thoroughly.

4 Remove the casserole from the oven and garnish with chopped parsley. Serve with the pasta.

4 large loin of lamb chops or 8 small ones

1 garlic clove, finely chopped

25 g (1 oz) butter

2 small courgettes, sliced

175 g (6 oz) button mushrooms, sliced

4 large tomatoes, skinned and sliced

1 tablespoon clear honey

150 ml (¼ pint) red wine

1 tablespoon chopped marjoram or 1 teaspoon dried marjoram

375 g (12 oz) wholewheat pasta

salt and pepper

1 tablespoon chopped parsley, to garnish

Serves 4

Preparation time: 15 minutes

Cooking time: 35 minutes

lamb chops with red wine sauce & pasta

asian-flavoured pappardelle

1 Bring a large saucepan of salted water to the boil. Add the pasta and cook for 8–12 minutes or according to the packet instructions, until just tender.

2 Meanwhile, heat a wok. Add the oil and heat over a moderate heat until hot. Add the meat and fry for 1 minute. Add the ginger and almost all of the spring onions and stir-fry for 2 minutes. Add the chilli, hoisin sauce, soy sauce, lime juice and rind and the coconut milk and cook for 1 minute.

3 Drain the pasta and turn into a large bowl. Fold in half of the meat and spoon into a large ovenproof dish. Spoon the remaining meat mixture over the dish and scatter with the rest of the spring onions. Cook in a preheated oven at 180°C (350°F), Gas Mark 4 for 10 minutes until the meat starts to crisp.

4 Remove the dish from the oven and scatter the coriander leaves over the top. Serve with lime wedges.

250 g (8 oz) pappardelle

2 tablespoons oil

375 g (12 oz) cooked duck, turkey or chicken

5 cm (2 inch) piece of fresh root ginger, peeled and finely chopped

1 bunch of spring onions, cut into long lengths

1 fresh red chilli, deseeded and chopped

3 tablespoons hoisin sauce

good splash of dark soy sauce

juice and rind of 1 lime

300 ml (½ pint) coconut milk

salt

coriander leaves, to garnish

lime wedges, to serve

Serves 6

Preparation time: 10 minutes

Cooking time: 20–25 minutes

68

1 Place the peppers in a saucepan with the onion, tomatoes and a pinch of salt, cover and simmer for about 5 minutes. Add the stock, bring to the boil and simmer for a further 15 minutes.

2 Meanwhile, bring a large saucepan of salted water to the boil. Add the pasta and cook for 8–12 minutes or according to the packet instructions, until just tender. Drain thoroughly.

3 Sprinkle the basil over the pepper sauce, adjust the seasoning to taste, then mix with the drained pasta and the diced mozzarella. Transfer to a large greased ovenproof dish, pour over the milk and cook in a preheated oven at 200°C (400°F), Gas Mark 6 for 15 minutes or until golden brown. Serve garnished with shredded basil leaves.

2 large yellow peppers, cored, deseeded and finely chopped

½ onion, thinly sliced

6 plum tomatoes, skinned and chopped

250 ml (8 fl oz) vegetable stock

375 g (12 oz) penne or other pasta shapes

½ teaspoon chopped basil

200 g (7 oz) mozzarella cheese, diced

3 tablespoons milk

salt and pepper

shredded basil leaves, to garnish

Serves 4

Preparation time: 20 minutes

Cooking time: 35–40 minutes

baked pasta with pepper sauce

1 Grill the pepper under a preheated hot grill, turning occasionally, until it is blistered and charred on all sides. Place in a plastic bag and leave until cool enough to handle. Strip off the skin and chop the flesh.

2 Heat the oil in a large saucepan, add the chopped pepper and garlic and cook for 3 minutes, stirring. Add the tomatoes, anchovies, wine and sugar, and season with pepper. Simmer for 15–20 minutes until thickened.

3 Meanwhile, bring a large saucepan of salted water to the boil. Add the pasta and cook for 8–12 minutes or according to the packet instructions, until just tender. Drain thoroughly.

4 To serve, divide the rigatoni between 4 warmed serving dishes and top with the sauce. Garnish with Parmesan and chopped parsley.

1 red pepper

4 tablespoons olive oil

2 garlic cloves, finely chopped

6 tomatoes, skinned and chopped

50 g (2 oz) canned anchovy fillets, rinsed and finely chopped

4 tablespoons dry white wine

1 teaspoon demerara sugar

375 g (12 oz) rigatoni

salt and pepper

To Garnish:

grated Parmesan cheese

chopped parsley

| **Serves 4** |
| **Preparation time:** 25 minutes |
| **Cooking time:** 25–30 minutes |

rigatoni with anchovy sauce

liver stroganoff

1   Melt the butter in a pan, add the onion and cook over a low heat until soft. Add the liver and cook for 5 minutes, stirring constantly.

2   Stir in the mushrooms, tomato purée, Worcestershire sauce, lemon juice and salt and pepper to taste then cook for a further 5 minutes, stirring occasionally.

3   Bring a large saucepan of salted water to the boil. Add the pasta and cook for 8–12 minutes or according to the packet instructions, until just tender. Drain thoroughly.

4   Remove the liver pan from the heat. Stir the cream into the pan, return the pan to a low heat and warm through without boiling. Taste and adjust the seasoning then serve with the pasta.

25 g (1 oz) butter

1 onion, chopped

500 g (1 lb) lamb's liver, sliced into very thin strips

250 g (8 oz) button mushrooms, sliced

1 tablespoon tomato purée

1 tablespoon Worcestershire sauce

4 tablespoons lemon juice

250 g (8 oz) pasta twists

150 ml (¼ pint) soured cream

salt and pepper

Serves 4

Preparation time: 15 minutes

Cooking time: 15–20 minutes

spicy beef bake

1 Bring a large saucepan of salted water to the boil. Add the pasta and cook for 8–12 minutes or according to the packet instructions, until just tender.

2 Meanwhile, heat the oil in a frying pan, add the shallots, cumin and chilli and cook for 2 minutes, stirring. Add the beef and cook over a high heat for 5 minutes, turning constantly. Stir in the chopped coriander. Add the chickpeas, lentils, tomato purée and mesquite sauce. Simmer for 2 minutes.

3 Drain the pasta and return it to the saucepan. Toss in a little oil. Stir the meat mixture into the pasta, then transfer it to a buttered 1.8 litre (3 pint) ovenproof dish. Sprinkle with the grated Emmental and cook in a preheated oven at 180°C (350°F), Gas Mark 4 for 25 minutes.

250 g (8 oz) three-colour farfalle

2 tablespoons oil, plus extra for tossing the pasta

2 shallots, finely chopped

pinch of ground cumin

1 dried chilli

250 g (8 oz) lean minced beef

50–75 g (2–3 oz) fresh coriander, chopped

425 g (14 oz) can chickpeas, drained

425 g (14 oz) can lentils, drained

2 tablespoons tomato purée

250 g (8 oz) jar mesquite sauce

75 g (3 oz) Emmental cheese, grated

Serves 6
Preparation time: 10 minutes
Cooking time: 40 minutes

■ Mesquite sauce is a hot, spicy sauce with a smoky flavour which hails from Mexico and Texas. It is named after the mesquite tree, whose wood is used for smoking and barbecueing foods.

seafood pasta with ginger

1   Place the mussels in a large saucepan. Scatter the ginger slices, shallots and half of the garlic over the top and sprinkle with the wine. Cover and steam over medium-high heat for about 5 minutes until the mussels open. Discard the ginger slices. Remove the mussels with a slotted spoon. Pour the cooking juices into a small saucepan. Cook over a high heat until the liquid is reduced to 125 ml (4 fl oz). Cover and set aside. Remove the mussels from their shells and set aside.

2   Bring a large saucepan of salted water to the boil. Add the pasta and cook for 8–12 minutes or according to the packet instructions, until just tender. Drain the pasta and transfer to a warmed serving dish.

3   Heat a wok over a moderate heat. When it is hot, add the oil and butter, then add the remaining garlic and the shredded ginger and cook for 30 seconds until softened. Add the prawns and cook for about 1 minute until they just begin to turn pink. Add the scallops and toss to mix.

4   Pour in the reserved cooking juices and the cream or crème fraîche then cook for about 1 minute until the sauce is reduced to a creamy consistency. Add the reserved mussels and lemon juice, and season with salt and pepper. Spoon over the pasta and serve at once, garnished with the deep-fried basil.

1 kg (2 lb) fresh mussels, cleaned

4 slices of fresh root ginger, peeled, plus 2 tablespoons finely shredded ginger

2 shallots, finely chopped

2 garlic cloves, finely chopped

125 ml (4 fl oz) dry white wine

375 g (12 oz) tagliarini

1 tablespoon olive oil

25 g (1 oz) unsalted butter

250 g (8 oz) raw prawns, peeled and deveined

250 g (8 oz) small scallops

125 ml (4 fl oz) double cream or crème fraîche

1–2 teaspoons lemon juice

salt and pepper

deep-fried basil leaves, to garnish

Serves 4–6

Preparation time: 20 minutes

Cooking time: 25 minutes

baked stuffed mushrooms •

ginger & carrot pasta ribbons •

deep-fried pasta •

prawn & apricot pasta salad •

green salad with walnuts & parmesan •

warm scallop & rocket salad •

chicken & mushroom penne salad •

pasta salad niçoise •

tuscan panzanella •

goats' cheese & watercress conchiglie •

crunchy pasta salad •

seafood sauce •

italian vegetable sauce •

sauce alla amatriciana •

coriander & walnut sauce •

fresh tomato sauce •

salads, sauces & side dishes

1 Bring a large saucepan of salted water to the boil. Add the pasta and cook for 8–12 minutes or according to the packet instructions, until just tender. Drain thoroughly.

2 Chop the mushroom stalks finely and set aside. Peel the mushrooms if blemished, and grill under a moderate heat for 5 minutes until just softened. Remove and set aside.

3 Put the chopped onion into a large bowl. Add the chopped mushroom stalks, cooked macaroni, walnuts, parsley, Cheddar cubes and tomato purée. Mix well, then add enough of the beaten egg to bind the mixture. Season to taste with salt and pepper.

4 Divide the filling between the mushrooms, mounding the mixture up with a spoon. Drizzle a little olive oil over them. Arrange the filled mushrooms, well apart, on a grill pan. Grill for 15–20 minutes until the top of the stuffing is crisp and has started to char at the edges. Serve at once, garnished with lemon wedges.

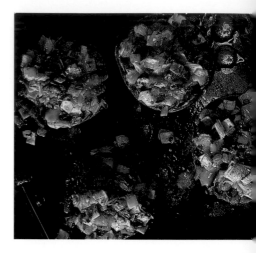

50 g (2 oz) short-cut macaroni

4 large field mushrooms

1 small onion, very finely chopped

25 g (1 oz) walnuts, chopped

1 tablespoon chopped parsley

25 g (1 oz) Cheddar cheese, cubed

1 tablespoon tomato purée

1 egg, beaten

1 tablespoon olive oil

salt and pepper

lemon wedges, to garnish

Serves 4
Preparation time: 10 minutes
Cooking time: 25–30 minutes

baked stuffed mushrooms

ginger & carrot pasta ribbons

1 Bring a large saucepan of salted water to the boil. Add the pasta and cook for 8–12 minutes or according to the packet instructions, until just tender.

2 Meanwhile, using a potato peeler, shave the carrots into thin ribbons. Either melt the butter in a frying pan and sauté the carrots and ginger for 5 minutes or steam them without the butter until tender.

3 Drain the pasta and return it to the rinsed-out pan. Toss with the oil and season with pepper. Carefully fold the carrot mixture into the cooked pasta. Sprinkle with pine nuts and serve at once.

300 g (10 oz) pappardelle or other broad egg noodles

2 carrots

25 g (1 oz) butter (optional)

2.5 cm (1 inch) piece fresh root ginger, peeled and grated

2 tablespoons olive oil

25 g (1 oz) pine nuts

salt and pepper

Serves 4

Preparation time: 10 minutes

Cooking time: 8–12 minutes

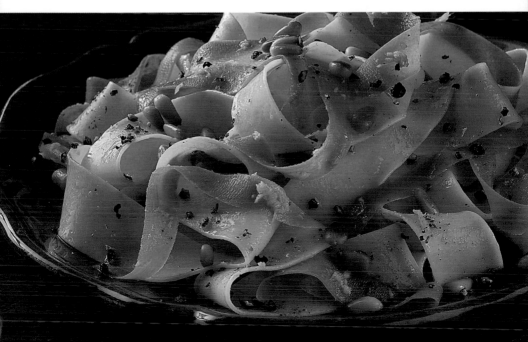

1 Dissolve the yeast and sugar in a little water. Set aside for 10 minutes.

2 Sift the flour and a little salt on to a work surface. Stir in the yeast mixture, then add the butter and enough stock to make a soft dough. Knead well, then roll out to a fairly thick sheet on a lightly-floured surface.

3 Fold the 4 corners of the dough in towards the centre, then flatten with the rolling pin. Fold and flatten again at least 5 more times. Roll out to a sheet about 5 mm (¼ inch) thick and cut into small rectangles.

4 Heat the oil and deep fry the shapes a few at a time until golden brown and puffed up. Drain on kitchen paper while frying the remainder. Sprinkle with salt and pepper and serve hot.

½ teaspoon dried yeast

¼ teaspoon sugar

500 g (1 lb) plain flour

25 g (1 oz) butter

150 ml (¼ pint) lukewarm chicken stock

vegetable oil, for deep frying

salt and pepper

Serves 6

Preparation time: 30 minutes, plus resting

Cooking time: 20–30 minutes

deep-fried pasta

■ These crisp, tasty puffs make excellent nibbles with drinks, and are ideal to serve with savoury sauces and dips.

prawn & apricot
pasta salad

1 Bring a large saucepan of salted
water to the boil. Add the pasta
and cook for 8–12 minutes or
according to the packet instructions,
until just tender. Drain, refresh with
cold water and drain again.

2 To make the dressing, mix the
yogurt, mayonnaise, grated
cucumber and mint. Season with salt
and pepper to taste.

3 Mix the cold pasta with the
prawns, apricot and cucumber
slices. Fold in the dressing, chill lightly,
then serve garnished with mint sprigs.

250 g (8 oz) conchiglie

125 g (4 oz) cooked peeled prawns

4 fresh apricots, peeled, stoned and
sliced

¼ cucumber, halved and thinly sliced

mint sprigs, to garnish

Dressing:

3 tablespoons natural yogurt

3 tablespoons mayonnaise

3 tablespoons grated cucumber

3 teaspoons chopped mint

salt and pepper

Serves 4

Preparation time: 15 minutes

Cooking time: 8–12 minutes

green salad with walnuts & parmesan

1 If the salad leaves are large tear them roughly, and place them in a serving bowl with the onion.

2 In a dry pan, lightly toast the walnut pieces, then roughly chop them and leave to cool.

3 To make the dressing, either whisk all the ingredients together in a small bowl or place in a screw-top jar and shake until blended.

4 Add the walnuts to the salad and pour over the dressing. Toss lightly to mix. Use a small sharp knife to slice the Parmesan into very thin shavings. Sprinkle these over the salad and serve at once.

large bowl of mixed salad leaves, (for example, rocket, corn salad, spring cabbage, red oak leaf, frisée, chicory)

½ mild onion, chopped

50 g (2 oz) walnut pieces

40 g (1½ oz) piece Parmesan cheese

Dressing:

5 tablespoons walnut oil

2 tablespoons red wine vinegar

½–1 teaspoon wholegrain mustard

pinch of sugar

salt and pepper

Serves 4–6
Preparation time: 10 minutes
Cooking time: 2–3 minutes

1   In a small bowl, combine the lemon juice and 2 tablespoons of the oil. Season to taste with salt and pepper. Set aside.

2   Heat the remaining oil in a frying pan over a moderate heat. Add the red peppers with a pinch of salt and cook for about 5 minutes, stirring, until just tender. Transfer the peppers to a plate and set aside. Arrange the salad leaves on individual plates.

3   Rinse the scallops and pat dry with kitchen paper. Season them with salt and pepper and arrange in one layer in the top of a steamer set over boiling water. Cover and steam over a high heat for about 3 minutes until tender. Drain on kitchen paper.

4   To serve, arrange the warm scallops on the salad leaves. Arrange the red peppers, olives, capers and chives around the scallops. Whisk the dressing and spoon it over the salad. Serve at once.

2 tablespoons lemon juice

3 tablespoons olive oil

2 red peppers, cored, deseeded and cut into thin strips

mixed salad leaves

375 g (12 oz) scallops

50 g (2 oz) pitted black olives, quartered

1 tablespoon capers

2 tablespoons snipped chives

salt and pepper

Serves 4

Preparation time: 10–15 minutes

Cooking time: 8 minutes

warm scallop & rocket salad

■ This salad would make a good starter before a light pasta main-course dish. Alternatively, serve with spaghetti dressed with a simple sauce.

84

chicken & mushroom penne salad

1 Bring a large saucepan of salted water to the boil. Add the pasta and cook for 8–12 minutes or according to the packet instructions, until just tender.

2 Drain the pasta, rinse under cold running water in a colander and drain again. Transfer the cooled pasta to a large salad bowl.

3 Add the chicken, mushrooms and red pepper, with the oil, sesame seeds, lemon juice and spring onions. Add salt and pepper to taste and toss well. Garnish with the chopped parsley.

300 g (10 oz) penne

250 g (8 oz) cooked chicken breast, sliced into strips

125 g (4 oz) button mushrooms, sliced

1 red pepper, cored, deseeded and finely sliced

2 tablespoons sesame oil

1 teaspoon sesame seeds

1 tablespoon lemon juice

4 spring onions, diagonally sliced

salt and pepper

2 tablespoons chopped parsley, to garnish

Serves 4

Preparation time: 15 minutes

Cooking time: 8–12 minutes

pasta salad niçoise

1 Soak the anchovies in milk for 20 minutes to remove excess salt. Bring a large saucepan of salted water to the boil. Add the pasta and cook for 8–12 minutes or according to packet instructions, until just tender. Drain, refresh in cold water, then drain again.

2 Meanwhile, cook the beans in salted boiling water for 3–4 minutes until tender. Drain, refresh in cold water, then drain again.

3 Whisk the dressing ingredients together in a bowl. Stir in the pasta and beans and mix well. Season with salt and pepper then leave to cool.

4 Add the tomatoes, tuna and herbs and fold in gently. Transfer to a serving platter. Drain and dry the anchovies and cut the fillets in half lengthways. Arrange the anchovies, eggs and olives over the top of the salad and serve at once.

50 g (2 oz) can anchovies in oil, drained

a little milk

250 g (8 oz) farfalle

250 g (8 oz) French beans, topped and tailed

2 firm ripe tomatoes, skinned and cut into wedges

200 g (7 oz) can tuna, drained and flaked

2 tablespoons chopped mixed herbs (for example, tarragon, basil, parsley)

2 hard-boiled eggs, shelled and quartered

50 g (2 oz) pitted black olives

salt and pepper

Dressing:

6 tablespoons olive oil

3 tablespoons tarragon vinegar

½ teaspoon mustard powder

pinch of sugar

Serves 4–6
Preparation time: 20 minutes
Cooking time: 8–12 minutes

tuscan panzanella

1   Scatter the bread cubes on a tray and leave them, uncovered, to harden overnight.

2   Put the tomatoes, cucumber, red pepper, onion, capers and parsley into a large non-metallic bowl and mix gently. In a small bowl, combine the vinegar, mustard, anchovies, if using, and oregano. Whisk in the oil. Season to taste with salt and pepper. Pour over the mixed vegetables and stir to mix. Cover and leave to stand at room temperature for at least 1 hour.

3   About 20 minutes before serving, mix the bread cubes with the vegetables. Taste and adjust the seasoning. To serve, transfer the salad to individual plates and garnish with parsley sprigs.

250 g (8 oz) Italian country bread, crusts removed, cut into 2.5 cm (1 inch) cubes

3 large ripe tomatoes, peeled, deseeded and chopped

1 cucumber, peeled, deseeded and diced

1 red pepper, cored, deseeded and diced

1 small red onion, thinly sliced

3 tablespoons capers

25 g (1 oz) chopped parsley

4 tablespoons red wine vinegar

4 tablespoons Dijon mustard

25 g (1 oz) anchovy fillets, finely chopped (optional)

2 teaspoons finely chopped oregano

250 ml (8 fl oz) olive oil

salt and pepper

parsley sprigs, to garnish

Serves 4–6

Preparation time: 15 minutes, plus standing

goats' cheese & watercress conchiglie

1 Bring a large saucepan of salted water to the boil. Add the pasta and cook for 8–12 minutes or according to the packet instructions, until just tender. Drain the pasta, rinse under cold running water in a colander and drain again. Transfer to a large salad bowl.

2 Mix the spring onions, raspberry vinegar and oil in a bowl. Add salt and pepper to taste. Pour the dressing over the pasta.

3 Fold in the goats' cheese, the orange or grapefruit slices and the watercress. Toss the salad and chill until required.

300 g (10 oz) conchiglie

3 spring onions, diagonally sliced

3 tablespoons raspberry vinegar

6 tablespoons olive oil

125 g (4 oz) soft goats' cheese, diced

1 orange or grapefruit, peeled and sliced into rings

1 bunch of watercress, washed and trimmed

salt and pepper

Serves 4	
Preparation time: 10 minutes	
Cooking time: 8–12 minutes	

crunchy pasta salad

1 Bring a large saucepan of salted water to the boil. Add the pasta and cook for 8–12 minutes or according to the packet instructions, until just tender.

2 Drain the pasta and rinse under cold running water in a colander. Drain again thoroughly and transfer to a large salad bowl. Add the cabbage and celery.

3 Quarter the apple, slice it into a bowl and sprinkle with lemon juice to prevent it from browning. Fold the apple slices into the pasta with the sultanas. Mix together the mayonnaise and milk, add salt and pepper to taste, then fold it into the salad. Garnish with the cayenne pepper and celery leaves.

300 g (10 oz) conchiglie
¼ red cabbage, shredded
2 celery sticks, chopped
1 Granny Smith apple, cored
1 tablespoon lemon juice
25 g (1 oz) sultanas
4 tablespoons mayonnaise
4 tablespoons milk
salt and pepper

To Garnish:
pinch of cayenne pepper
celery leaves

Serves 4

Preparation time: 20 minutes

Cooking time: 8–12 minutes

seafood sauce

1 Melt the butter or margarine in a saucepan, add the onion and garlic and cook gently for 2 minutes, stirring. Add the flour and stir over a low heat for 2 minutes. Gradually add the stock and the wine and bring to the boil, stirring or whisking constantly.

2 Reduce the heat and stir in the halibut and scallops and cook gently for 2–3 minutes.

3 Stir in the mussels, prawns and marjoram. Season to taste with salt and pepper and heat gently for 1 minute. Just before serving, add the cream and heat through.

50 g (2 oz) butter or margarine

1 onion, finely chopped

1 garlic clove, crushed

50 g (2 oz) plain flour

450 ml (¾ pint) vegetable or fish stock

150 ml (¼ pint) white wine

125 g (4 oz) halibut, cubed

6 scallops, cut into quarters

50 g (2 oz) canned or frozen mussels

125 g (4 oz) cooked peeled prawns

1 tablespoon chopped marjoram

150 ml (¼ pint) single cream

salt and pepper

Serves 4

Preparation time: 15 minutes

Cooking time: 10 minutes

1 tablespoon oil

1 onion, finely chopped

1 red pepper, cored, deseeded and finely chopped

1 yellow pepper, cored, deseeded and finely chopped

2 celery sticks, finely chopped

1 courgette, finely chopped

4 tomatoes, skinned, deseeded and chopped

250 g (8 oz) spinach leaves, chopped

150 ml (¼ pint) vegetable stock or water

1 teaspoon caster sugar

salt and pepper

1 Heat the oil in a large saucepan, add the onion, peppers, celery and courgette and cook for 2 minutes, stirring, until almost tender.

2 Stir in the tomatoes, spinach, stock or water and the sugar. Season to taste with salt and pepper.

3 Bring to the boil and cook for 10 minutes until the sauce has reduced and thickened.

Serves 4
Preparation time: 15 minutes
Cooking time: 15 minutes

italian vegetable sauce

■ This is a great sauce to make when summer vegetables are plentiful. Serve as a topping to plain pasta, or use for layering in lasagne and other baked pasta dishes.

sauce alla amatriciana

1 Heat the oil in a heavy saucepan, add the bacon and fry gently for 5 minutes until golden. Remove with a slotted spoon and keep warm.

2 In the same pan, fry the onion until transparent, then add the pimento, tomatoes and bacon. Season to taste with salt and pepper, then cook briskly for 10 minutes, stirring all the time. Serve hot over freshly cooked pasta, garnished with grated Parmesan or pecorino cheese and a coriander sprig.

1 tablespoon sunflower or olive oil

75 g (3 oz) lean unsmoked bacon, derinded and diced

1 small onion, finely chopped

1 canned pimento, chopped

375 g (12 oz) fresh tomatoes, skinned and chopped

salt and pepper

To Garnish:

grated Parmesan or pecorino cheese

fresh coriander sprigs

Serves 4	
Preparation time: 10 minutes	
Cooking time: 20 minutes	

coriander & walnut sauce

1 Place the olive oil and cream in a bowl.

2 Add the cheese, walnuts and chopped coriander. Season with salt and pepper and mix all the ingredients together thoroughly.

3 Pour over freshly cooked pasta and stir well to combine. Garnish with coriander sprigs and serve immediately.

1 tablespoon olive oil

50 ml (2 fl oz) double cream

25 g (1 oz) Cheddar cheese, grated

25 g (1 oz) walnuts, finely chopped

25 g (1 oz) fresh coriander, finely chopped, plus extra sprigs to garnish

salt and pepper

Serves 4

Preparation time: 5 minutes

■ This sauce can be made in advance and stored in the refrigerator in a covered container for 1-2 days.

1 tablespoon olive oil

1 celery stick, chopped

1 carrot, chopped

2 onions, chopped

2 garlic cloves, crushed

1 kg (2 lb) large ripe tomatoes, quartered

2 teaspoons caster sugar

2 tablespoons chopped basil

salt and pepper

1 Heat the oil in a saucepan, add the celery, carrot, onions and garlic and cook gently for 3 minutes, stirring, until tender.

2 Stir in the tomatoes, sugar, basil and salt and pepper to taste. Bring to the boil. Reduce the heat, cover the saucepan with a lid and cook gently for 30 minutes.

3 Transfer the sauce to a blender or food processor and process until smooth. Reheat and serve over freshly cooked pasta.

Serves 4–6
Preparation time: 10 minutes
Cooking time: 35 minutes

fresh tomato sauce

index